ABC
of PEOPLE and THINGS in the BIBLE
Child's Workbook
(Ages 6-8)

BY

© Oluwakemi O.Ola-Ojo 2011

ABC of People and Things in the Bible -
Child's Workbook 1.

ISBN – 978-1-908015-05-1
© 2011 by Oluwakemi O. Ola-Ojo

All publishing rights belong exclusively to Protokos Publishers.

Published by:
Protokos Publishers
PO Box 48424
London
SE15 2YL
United Kingdom
Website: www.protokospublishers.co.uk
E-Mail: admin@protokospublishers.co.uk

Cover design by **DM Audiovisuals**
www.dmaudiovisuals.com

Printed in the United Kingdom. All rights reserved under International Copyright Law. Contents and/or cover may not be reproduced in whole or in part in any form without the express written consent of the Publisher.

Introduction:

This is the 2nd of a 2-part series. Book one is for the parent/teacher and book two is for the child. We recommend teaching only an alphabet per week and conscious efforts should be made by the parent/teacher to do the exercise with the child all through the week. We need to train/teach the child line-by-line, precept upon precept. Every alphabet has been written up with some ideas. We would recommend that the parent/teacher uses only what is applicable for the child and pitch the teaching to the child's level of understanding.

In book two the same story is written in simple English for the child to read to the parent/teacher, the aim of which is to help him/her learn to read. The child can write, draw and colour what he/she has drawn. The reading could be done daily as the child's bedtime story. It is meant to reinforce what has been taught previously. Effectively this is the child's workbook.

Allow the child a break if he or she is tired while working on the workbook. Praise child for his or her effort, however little.

The parent/teacher should assess the child's performance in the reading, writing and drawing by ticking the most appropriate commendation at the end of the 'time to draw page'.

This workbook belongs to:

----

of address:

Date:_____ /_____ /20_____

Time to practice how to write.

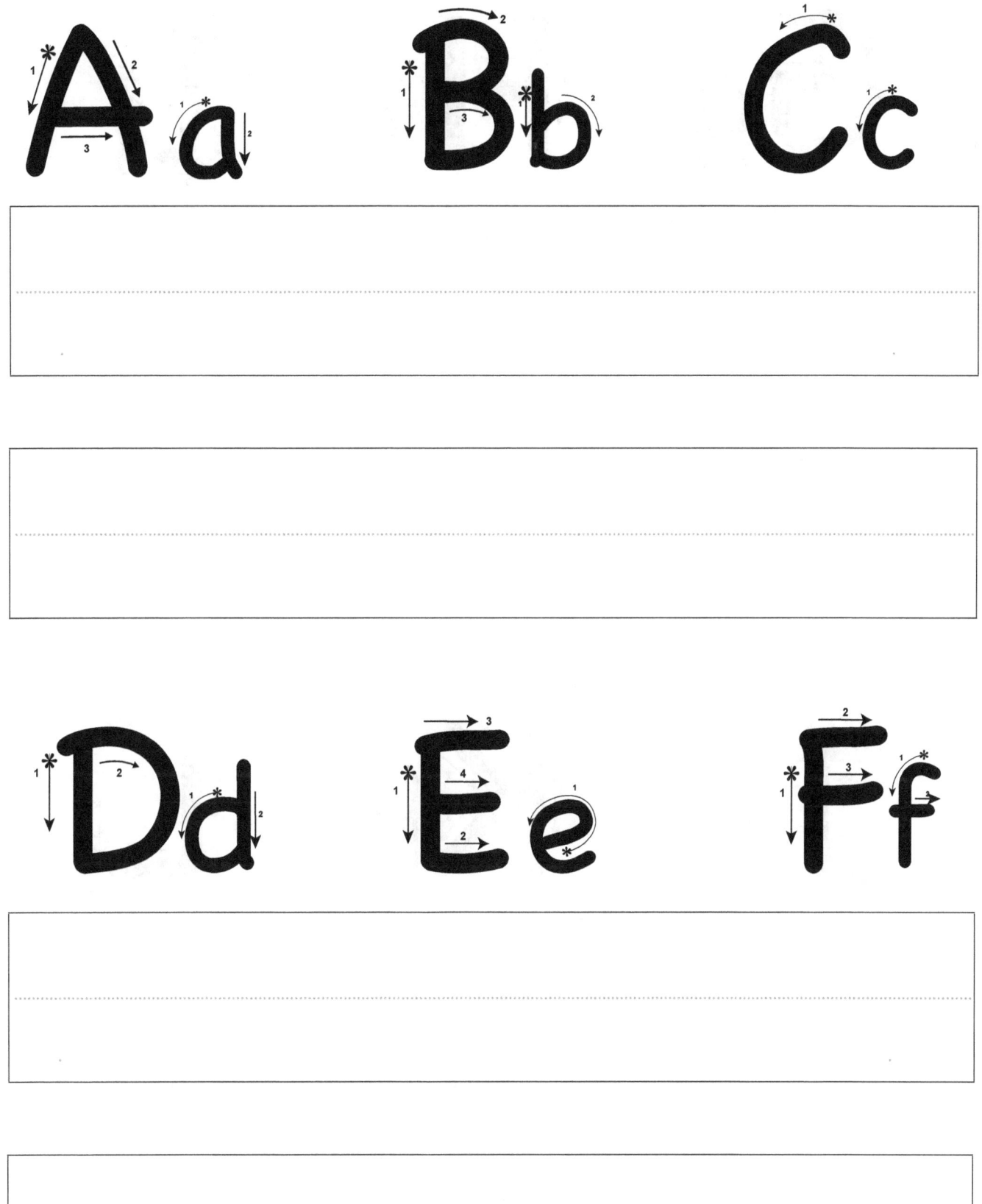

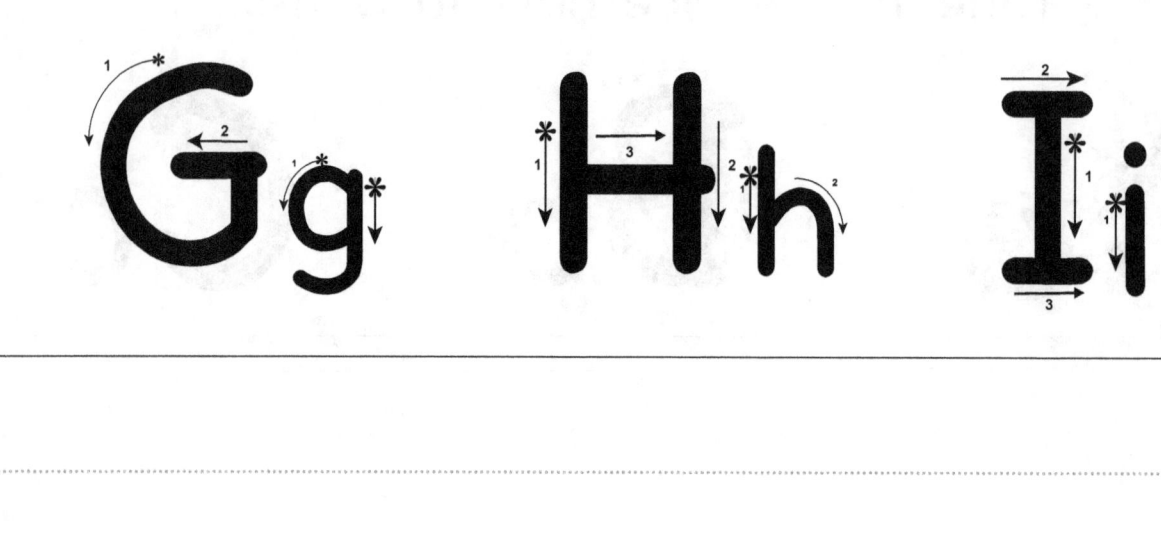

Pp Qq Rr

7

Ss Tt Uu

Vv Ww Xx

Time to read:

A is for Adam.
Adam's wife was Eve.
Adam had three sons.
Adam disobeyed God.
Adam was the first man on earth.
Adam named all the animals on earth.

Time to write:

A is for Adam.

A is for Adam.

Adam was the first man on earth.

Adam named all the animals on earth.

Time to draw:

Draw Adam in the garden.

Well done ☐
Good Job ☐
Excellent ☐

Time to read:

B is for Boaz.
Boaz had many fields.
Boaz was a wealthy man.
Boaz gave grains to Ruth.
Boaz later married Ruth.
Boaz was very kind to Ruth.

Time to write:

B is for Boaz.

B is for Boaz.

Boaz gave grains to Ruth.

Boaz was very kind to Ruth.

Time to draw:

Draw rich Boaz on the farm with wheat harvesters.

Well done □
Good Job □
Excellent □

Time to read:

C is for Caleb.
Caleb loved God.
Caleb was a brave man.
Caleb was one of twelve spies.
Caleb brought good report and trusted God.
Caleb and Joshua were allowed to get into Canaan.

Time to write:

C is for Caleb.

C is for Caleb.

Caleb and Joshua brought good report.

Caleb and Joshua got into Canaan.

Time to draw:

Draw Caleb speaking to the people.

Well done ☐
Good Job ☐
Excellent ☐

Time to read:

D is for David.
David loved God.
David played the harp.
David looked after the sheep.
David killed the bear and the lion.
David was one of the sons of Jesse.

Time to write:

D is for David.

| **D** is for David. |

| |

David killed the bear and the lion.

| |

| |

David was one of the sons of Jesse.

| |

| |

Time to draw:

Draw David as a shepherd boy.

Well done ☐
Good Job ☐
Excellent ☐

Time to read:

E is for Enoch.
Enoch loved God.
Enoch did not die.
Enoch was a good man.
Enoch rode on a chariot.
Enoch's chariot went to heaven.

Time to write:

E is for Enoch.

E is for Enoch.

Enoch rode on a chariot.

Enoch's chariot went to heaven.

Time to draw:

Draw Enoch on the chariot to heaven.

Well done ☐
Good Job ☐
Excellent ☐

Time to read:

F is for Felix.
Felix was a governor.
Felix lived in Caesarea.
Felix's wife was Drusilla.
Felix talked to Paul often.
Felix allowed Paul to have visitors in the prison.

Time to write:

F is for Felix.

F is for Felix.

Felix talked to Paul often.

Felix allowed Paul to have visitors.

Time to draw:

Draw Felix as a governor.

Well done ☐
Good Job ☐
Excellent ☐

Time to read:

G is for Goliath.
Goliath was a soldier.
Goliath was a brave man.
Goliath was a very tall man.
Goliath had six toes in each foot.
Goliath had six fingers in each hand.

Time to write:

G is for Goliath.

G is for Goliath.

Goliath had six toes in each foot.

Goliath had six fingers in each hand.

Time to draw:

Draw proud, tall Goliath on the battle field.

Well done ☐
Good Job ☐
Excellent ☐

Time to read:

H is for the Hannah.
Hannah loved God.
Hannah had no children.
Hannah prayed to God in the temple.
Hannah went home a happy woman.
Hannah later gave birth to Samuel.

Time to write:

H is for Hannah.

H is for Hannah.

Hannah prayed to God in the temple.

Hannah later gave birth to Samuel.

Time to draw:

Draw Hannah praying in the temple on her knees.

Well done ☐
Good Job ☐
Excellent ☐

Time to read:

I is for Isaac.
Isaac loved God.
Isaac's mother was Sarah.
Isaac's father was Abraham.
Isaac carried firewood for his father.
Isaac was the father of Esau and Jacob.

Time to write:

I is for Isaac.

I is for Isaac.

Isaac carried firewood for his father.

Isaac was the father of Esau and Jacob.

Time to draw:

Draw Isaac and his family.

Well done ☐
Good Job ☐
Excellent ☐

Time to read:

J is for Jesus Christ.
Jesus loved God.
Jesus obeyed God.
Jesus loves everyone.
Jesus healed everyone that was sick.
Jesus died and rose again on the third day.

Time to write:

J is for Jesus Christ.

| J is for Jesus Christ. |

| |

Jesus healed everyone that was sick.

| |

| |

Jesus rose again on the third day.

| |

| |

Time to draw:

Draw Jesus Christ healing the sick.

Well done ☐
Good Job ☐
Excellent ☐

Time to read:

K is for King Asa.
King Asa loved God.
King Asa obeyed God.
King Asa was king in Judah.
King Asa did all that was right.
King Asa was the son of king Abijah.

Time to write:

K is for King Asa.

K is for King Asa.

King Asa was king in Judah.

King Asa was the son of king Abijah.

Time to draw:

Draw a young King on the throne.

Well done ☐
Good Job ☐
Excellent ☐

Time to read:

L is for Lydia.
Lydia believed in God.
Lydia was from Thyatira.
Lydia fed Paul and Silas.
Lydia sold purple clothes.
Lydia went to the place of prayer.

Time to write:

L is for Lydia.

| L is for Lydia. |

| |

Lydia sold purple clothes.

| |

| |

Lydia went to the place of prayer.

| |

| |

Time to draw:

Draw Lydia as a seller of purple clothes.

Well done ☐
Good Job ☐
Excellent ☐

Time to read:

M is for Moses.
Moses' mother made him a basket.
Moses' mother put him in the basket on the river.
Moses was adopted by Pharaoh's daughter.
Moses grew up as a Prince in Egypt.
Moses led God's people out of Egypt.

Time to write:

M is for Moses.

M is for Moses.

Moses grew up as a Prince in Egypt.

Moses led God's people out of Egypt.

Time to draw:

Draw Baby Moses in the basket floating on the river.

Well done ☐
Good Job ☐
Excellent ☐

Time to read:

N is for Noah.
Noah was a good man.
Noah feared and obeyed God.
Noah built an ark for a long time.
Noah and his family went inside the ark.
Noah's ark floated when the rains came.

Time to write:

N is for Noah.

N is for Noah.

Noah and his family went inside the ark.

Noah's ark floated when the rains came.

Time to draw:

Draw Noah and animals in the ark.

Well done ☐
Good Job ☐
Excellent ☐

Time to read:

O is for Onesimus.
Onesimus was a slave.
Onesimus loved God.
Onesimus's master was Philemon.
Onesimus became a friend of Paul.
Onesimus took a letter from Paul to Philemon.

Time to write:

O is for Onesimus.

O is for Onesimus.

Onesimus became a friend of Paul.

Onesimus took a letter to Philemon.

Time to draw:

Draw Onesimus talking to Paul.

Well done ☐
Good Job ☐
Excellent ☐

Time to read:

P is for Peter.
Peter had a wife.
Peter had brothers.
Peter was a fisherman.
Peter later followed Jesus.
Peter gave Jesus his boat to use.

Time to write:

P is for Peter.

P is for Peter.

Peter was a fisherman.

Peter gave Jesus his boat to use.

Time to draw:

Draw Peter in the boat fishing.

Well done ☐
Good Job ☐
Excellent ☐

Time to read:

Q is for Queen of Sheba.
Queen of Sheba ruled over Sheba.
Queen of Sheba travelled to Jerusalem.
Queen of Sheba listened to King Solomon's wise advice.
Queen of Sheba gave a lot of presents to King Solomon.
Queen of Sheba later returned home to her people.

Time to write:

Q is for Queen of Sheba.

Q is for **Q**ueen of **S**heba.

Queen of Sheba listened to King Solomon.

Queen of Sheba later returned home.

Time to draw:

Draw queen of Sheba with her wealth on her way to Israel.

Well done ☐
Good Job ☐
Excellent ☐

Time to read:

R is for Rebecca.
Rebecca was Bethuel's daughter.
Rebecca was the wife of Isaac.
Rebecca was a very good cook.
Rebecca was the mother of twins.
Rebecca's sons were Esau and Jacob.

Time to write:

R is for Rebecca.

R is for Rebecca.

Rebecca was the mother of twins.

Rebecca's sons were Esau and Jacob.

Time to draw:

Draw Rebecca holding her twins.

Well done ☐
Good Job ☐
Excellent ☐

Time to read:

S is for Shepherds.
Shepherds look after the sheep.
Shepherds know where the good waters are.
Shepherds know where the good grasses are.
Shepherds protect their sheep from wild animals.
Shepherds watch over their sheep at night in the fields.

Time to write:

S is for Shepherds.

S is for Shepherds.

Shepherds protect their sheep.

Shepherds watch over their sheep always.

Time to draw:

Draw shepherds in the field with their flock at night.

Well done ☐
Good Job ☐
Excellent ☐

Time to read:

T is for Timothy.
Timothy's mother was Eunice.
Timothy's grandmother was Lois.
Timothy was taught by his mother and grandma.
Timothy loved God like his mother and grandma.
Timothy later became a Pastor and was loved by Paul.

Time to write:

T is for Timothy.

T is for Timothy.

Timothy was taught by two women.

Timothy later became a Pastor.

Time to draw:

Draw Timothy with a Bible in his hands.

Well done ☐
Good Job ☐
Excellent ☐

Time to read:

U is for Uriah.
Uriah was a brave man.
Uriah's wife was Bathsbeba.
Uriah feared and loved God.
Uriah was a soldier in David's army.
Uriah defended his nation in battles.

Time to write:

U is for Uriah.

U is for Uriah.

Uriah was a soldier in David's army.

Uriah defended his nation in battles.

Time to draw:

Draw Uriah as a soldier.

Well done ☐
Good Job ☐
Excellent ☐

Time to read:

V is for Virgin Mary.
Virgin Mary loved God.
Virgin Mary believed in God.
Virgin Mary's cousin was Elizabeth.
Virgin Mary was visited by the angel.
Virgin Mary was the mother of Jesus Christ.

Time to write:

V is for Virgin Mary.

V is for Virgin Mary.

Virgin Mary's cousin was Elizabeth.

Virgin Mary was the mother of Jesus.

Time to draw:

Draw Virgin Mary talking to the angel.

Well done ☐
Good Job ☐
Excellent ☐

Time to read:

W is for the wise men.
Wise men from the East saw a star in the sky.
Wise men knew the star announced the birth of a king.
Wise men came to search for the newborn king.
Wise men brought many nice gifts for the baby king.
Wise men found baby Jesus in a manger in Bethlehem.

Time to write:

W is for wise men.

W is for wise men.

Wise men brought gifts for baby Jesus.

Wise men found baby Jesus in a manger.

Time to draw:

Draw Wise men with their gifts.

Well done ☐
Good Job ☐
Excellent ☐

Time to read:

X is for X-Ray.
X-ray can help to see inside a person's body.
X-ray can help to see a person's lungs and heart.
X-ray can help to see a broken bone in the body.
X-ray can help to see if a person is sick inside the body.
God alone can see what is in a person's heart and mind.

Time to write:

X is for X-Ray.

X is for X-Ray.

X-ray can see inside a person's body.

God can see what is in a person's mind.

Time to draw:

Draw a Chest X-ray.

Well done ☐
Good Job ☐
Excellent ☐

Time to read:

Y is for YAWEH.
Yahweh created the entire world.
Yahweh is in control of the world.
Yahweh is one of the names of God.
Yahweh created every living and non-living thing.
Yahweh loves and knows everyone and everything.

Time to write:

Y is for Yaweh.

Y is for Yaweh.

Yahweh created the entire world.

Yahweh is in control of the entire world.

Time to draw:

Draw heaven and a throne or a beautiful sky.

Well done ☐
Good Job ☐
Excellent ☐

Time to read:

Z is for Zacchaeus.
Zacchaeus was a tax collector.
Zacchaeus wanted to see Jesus.
Zacchaeus was a very short man.
Zacchaeus climbed the tree to see Jesus.
Zacchaeus and his family believed in Jesus.

Time to write:

Z is for Zacchaeus.

Z is for Zacchaeus.

Zacchaeus wanted to see Jesus.

Zacchaeus was a very short man.

Time to draw:

Draw short Zacchaeus on a tree with Jesus and some people coming on the road.

Well done ☐
Good Job ☐
Excellent ☐

How to become God's child and friend:

Please say this prayer:

Dear Lord, thank You for my life. I am sorry for all the bad things that I have said or done. Please forgive me for all these bad things.

Lord, I want to be Your child and friend from now on. Please come into my heart and forgive me for all the bad things that I have said and done. From now, please be my Lord and Friend and teach me Your ways in Jesus name I pray. Amen

Coming out Soon

- **A.B.C. OF PEOPLE AND THINGS IN THE BIBLE** *(Parent/Teacher Manual 1)*

- **A.B.C. OF PEOPLE AND THINGS IN THE BIBLE BOOK 2**

- **A.B.C. OF PLACES IN THE BIBLE BOOKS 1 & 2**

www.ingramcontent.com/pod-product-compliance
Lightning Source LLC
Chambersburg PA
CBHW081126080526
44587CB00021B/3765